LIFE
QUESTIONS

Quarto

© 2023 Quarto Publishing Group USA Inc.

This edition published in 2023 by Chartwell Books,
an imprint of The Quarto Group
142 West 36th Street, 4th Floor
New York, NY 10018 USA
T (212) 779-4972 F (212) 779-6058
www.Quarto.com

Contains content originally published as *This is Me* in 2021, *3001 Questions About Me* in 2022 and *3001 Would You Rather Questions* in 2022 by Chartwell Books.

10 9 8 7 6 5 4 3 2 1

Chartwell titles are also available at discount for retail, wholesale, promotional, and bulk purchase. For details, contact the Special Sales Manager by email at specialsales@quarto.com or by mail at The Quarto Group, Attn: Special Sales Manager, 100 Cummings Center Suite 265D, Beverly, MA 01915, USA.

ISBN: 978-0-7858-4382-5

Publisher: Wendy Friedman
Senior Managing Editor: Meredith Mennitt
Senior Design Manager: Michael Caputo
Editor: Cathy Davis
Designer: Kate Sinclair

All stock photos and design elements ©Shutterstock

Printed in China

LIFE QUESTIONS

Reflect and explore your
past, present & future

chartwell
books

Introduction

Take a break from social media and screens with *Life Questions*. Whether you're a seasoned writer or looking for a new creative outlet, this book is for you! Use it to record your thoughts or to practice self-reflection.

The questions and prompts are divided into three sections, each one focused on your present, past, and future. Record your current favorites, reminisce about your most significant childhood memories, and start dreaming and planning for your future.

Be honest. If you can't be honest with yourself then who can you be honest with? These questions are meant to be thought-provoking and provide insight. But don't overthink your answers. No one else will read them.

There are no rules on how to complete this book. Work through the pages in order or turn to a random page when you feel like writing. When you're finished, keep this book, and then come back to it in the future. You may find some of your answers change over time. Reflect on what you've learned and celebrate your growth.

Start writing today!

About Me

"To be yourself in a world that is constantly trying to make you something else is the greatest accomplishment."

—RALPH WALDO EMERSON

What brings you joy?

_____

_____

_____

_____

_____

_____

What's your favorite place on earth?

_____

_____

_____

_____

_____

_____

Do you like or dislike conflict? Why?

_____

_____

_____

_____

_____

_____

Are you an outdoors kind of person?

_____
_____
_____
_____
_____
_____
_____

Do you have any habits that are both good and bad?

_____
_____
_____
_____
_____
_____
_____

What's your definition of beauty?

_____
_____
_____
_____
_____
_____
_____

How would you describe your parents?

_____

_____

_____

_____

_____

_____

_____

_____

_____

_____

How do you feel today?

_____

_____

_____

_____

_____

_____

_____

_____

_____

_____

What's the thing you're least afraid of?

_____

_____

_____

_____

_____

_____

_____

_____

_____

What effect do you have on people?

_____

_____

_____

_____

_____

_____

_____

_____

_____

_____

When you go out, how do you like to dress?

_____

_____

_____

_____

_____

_____

_____

_____

_____

_____

When you wake up, what's the first thing you think about?

_____

_____

_____

_____

_____

_____

_____

_____

_____

_____

What's the worst argument you've ever been in?

_____

_____

_____

_____

_____

_____

_____

_____

_____

What's the last thing you learned that blew you away?

_____

_____

_____

_____

_____

_____

_____

_____

_____

_____

Rapid Fire

Quick! Pick your favorite of these duos. No thinking – go with your first impulse.

	OR	
Salty		Sweet
Dog		Cat
Hug		Kiss
Fiction		Nonfiction
Coffee		Tea
Spring		Fall
Pencils		Pen
Silver		Gold
Checkers		Chess
Star		Planet
Sheep		Goat
Vampire		Werewolf
Ocean		Mountain
Ketchup		Mustard
Movie		TV
Early Bird		Night Owl
Create		Destroy

Changing Tastes

Fill in your favorites at different stages of your life

	CHILD	TEEN	NOW
Favorite Song			
Favorite Person			
Favorite Hobby			
Favorite Color			
Favorite Movie			
Favorite Food			
Favorite Vice			
Favorite Celebrity			

What do you consider to be a success?

_____

_____

_____

_____

_____

_____

_____

What sounds do you like and dislike the most?

_____

_____

_____

_____

_____

_____

_____

What is something that always takes your breath away?

_____

_____

_____

_____

_____

_____

_____

What smells do you like and dislike the most?

How do you blow off steam?

What do you value most in a friendship?

What is something that doesn't affect you but affects others?

Do you like when people help you? Or do you prefer to do things alone?

Do you love yourself?

_____

_____

_____

_____

_____

_____

_____

_____

What's your biggest fear?

_____

_____

_____

_____

_____

_____

_____

_____

_____

_____

How did you sleep last night?

_____

_____

_____

_____

_____

_____

_____

_____

_____

What do you like most about yourself?

_____

_____

_____

_____

_____

_____

_____

_____

_____

_____

What are you most confident in when it comes to who you are?

_____

_____

_____

_____

_____

_____

_____

_____

_____

What are you most insecure about?

_____

_____

_____

_____

_____

_____

_____

_____

_____

_____

_____

Would You Rather?

Play it safe and have regrets **OR** take chances and have no regrets?

Live forever with little energy **OR** have a lot of energy but only a few months to live?

Walk for a mile on your hands **OR** crawl for a mile on your knees?

Be good at what you hate **OR** bad at what you love?

Have no emotions **OR** have no taste?

Have dinner with your favorite author **OR** your favorite singer?

Build a sandcastle **OR** a snow fort?

Live in Alaska for free **OR** in Hawaii for 10% over the normal cost?

Be a famous college athlete **OR** an unknown pro athlete?

Never sleep with a blanket **OR** never sleep with a pillow

Sleep on a bed of nails **OR** on a bed of coals?

Milkshakes **OR** root beer floats?

Bathe in sour milk **OR** shower in nacho cheese?

Lose your sense of smell **OR** sense of taste?

	OR	
Get trapped in a maze		in a cave?
New clothes		new shoes?
Cook dinner		wash the dishes?
Sort and wash the laundry		fold and put away the laundry?
Bump your head		stub your toe?
Party with people you hate		sit home alone?
Start your own business		buy someone else's business?
Super speed		super hearing?
Meet a talking scarecrow		a singing lion?
Have a food fight		a snowball fight?
Never have to wait in line		never have to search for a parking space?
Travel at the speed of light		travel at the speed of sound?
Tell ghost stories		have ghosts tell stories about you?
Be able to predict the future		fix the past?

How would your best friend describe you?

_____

_____

_____

_____

_____

_____

_____

How would your arch nemesis describe you?

_____

_____

_____

_____

_____

_____

_____

How would your pet describe you?

_____

_____

_____

_____

_____

_____

_____

How would your 3rd grade teacher describe you?

_____

_____

_____

_____

_____

_____

How would your favorite author describe you?

_____

_____

_____

_____

_____

_____

How do you describe yourself?

_____

_____

_____

_____

_____

_____

What do you do to relax?

_____

_____

_____

_____

_____

_____

_____

_____

_____

_____

Do you hide your emotions well?

_____

_____

_____

_____

_____

_____

_____

_____

_____

_____

_____

How do you define love?

_____

_____

_____

_____

_____

_____

_____

_____

_____

_____

What's your favorite decade? Why?

_____

_____

_____

_____

_____

_____

_____

_____

_____

_____

_____

_____

How do you reward yourself?

_____

_____

_____

_____

_____

_____

_____

_____

_____

Have you ever been ashamed of something?

_____

_____

_____

_____

_____

_____

_____

_____

_____

_____

_____

What's one thing you need to do every day?

_____

_____

_____

_____

_____

_____

_____

_____

_____

_____

What's your main source of stress-relief?

_____

_____

_____

_____

_____

_____

_____

_____

_____

_____

Confessions

What are your 5 deepest, darkest, most sinister or embarrassing secrets? You are going to destroy this after you are finished so get these confessions off your chest now.

1.

2.

3.

4.

5.

Point of Pride

List your top five biggest achievements and accomplishments.

1.
_____
_____
_____

2.
_____
_____
_____

3.
_____
_____
_____

4.
_____
_____
_____

5.
_____
_____
_____

Have you ever been depressed?

_____

_____

_____

_____

_____

_____

_____

_____

_____

_____

Do you judge people easily?

_____

_____

_____

_____

_____

_____

_____

_____

_____

_____

_____

What's the nicest thing anyone has ever done for you?

_____

_____

_____

_____

_____

_____

_____

_____

_____

If you were to write a novel, what would it be about?

_____

_____

_____

_____

_____

_____

_____

_____

_____

_____

_____

What's your favorite thing in a coffee shop?

_____

_____

_____

_____

_____

_____

_____

_____

_____

_____

What would you want to bring with you to a deserted island?

_____

_____

_____

_____

_____

_____

_____

_____

_____

_____

Have you ever been kind to a stranger?

_____

_____

_____

_____

_____

_____

_____

_____

When are you the most tired?

_____

_____

_____

_____

_____

_____

_____

_____

_____

_____

If you were asked to be on a reality show, would you say yes?

_____

_____

_____

_____

_____

_____

_____

_____

What's your morning wake-up routine?

_____

_____

_____

_____

_____

_____

_____

_____

_____

If you had a superpower, what would it be? Why?

_____

_____

_____

_____

_____

_____

_____

_____

_____

_____

What do you consider to be a good life?

_____

_____

_____

_____

_____

_____

_____

_____

_____

_____

_____

Three Words

Write down the first three words that come to mind when reading
the words below.

Today

1.	
2.	
3.	

Memory

1.	
2.	
3.	

Love

1.	
2.	
3.	

Money

1.
2.
3.

Family

1.
2.
3.

Home

1.
2.
3.

What's your relationship to money?

_____

_____

_____

_____

_____

_____

_____

_____

_____

If you could make one law, what would it be?

_____

_____

_____

_____

_____

_____

_____

_____

_____

_____

What's the first thing you notice when you meet someone?

_____

_____

_____

_____

_____

_____

_____

_____

_____

What are your worst three habits?

_____

_____

_____

_____

_____

_____

_____

_____

_____

_____

_____

What are you grateful for?

_____

_____

_____

_____

_____

_____

_____

_____

_____

_____

Have you ever broken up with someone?

_____

_____

_____

_____

_____

_____

_____

_____

_____

_____

_____

What do you love learning about?

_____

_____

_____

_____

_____

_____

_____

_____

_____

Who are the people you always ask for advice?

_____

_____

_____

_____

_____

_____

_____

_____

_____

_____

Favorite Things

List your top five favorite things about your life right now.

1.

2.

3.

4.

5.

Life Changes

ABOUT ME

List the top five things you want to change in your life.

1. _____

   _____

   _____

2. _____

   _____

   _____

3. _____

   _____

   _____

4. _____

   _____

   _____

5. _____

   _____

   _____

What is something you will always defend?

_____

_____

_____

_____

_____

_____

_____

_____

_____

_____

What will always make you laugh?

_____

_____

_____

_____

_____

_____

_____

_____

_____

_____

Where have you traveled to that personifies your best qualities?

_____

_____

_____

_____

_____

_____

_____

_____

_____

_____

How do you deal with disappointment?

_____

_____

_____

_____

_____

_____

_____

_____

_____

_____

_____

What's the one thing you would never do?

_____

_____

_____

_____

_____

_____

_____

_____

_____

Have you ever thought you were in love but then realized you weren't?

_____

_____

_____

_____

_____

_____

_____

_____

_____

Do you have a hobby? If not, what would it be?

_____

_____

_____

_____

_____

_____

_____

_____

_____

_____

Do you consider yourself good at adapting?

_____

_____

_____

_____

_____

_____

_____

_____

_____

_____

What's the wildest thing you've done?

When you hear birds singing, what do you think about?

What are you the perfect mixture of?

_____

_____

_____

_____

_____

_____

_____

_____

_____

_____

What is the one thing that can always cheer you up?

_____

_____

_____

_____

_____

_____

_____

_____

_____

_____

_____

_____

True or False

You like the spotlight.

TRUE	FALSE

You're good at directions and reading maps.

TRUE	FALSE

You can speak more than one language.

TRUE	FALSE

You show your emotions easily.

TRUE	FALSE

You're a people person.

TRUE	FALSE

You love trying new things.

TRUE	FALSE

You're often late to everything.

TRUE	FALSE

You're flexible.

TRUE	FALSE

You're self-critical.

TRUE	FALSE

You're goal oriented.

TRUE	FALSE

You love sports.

TRUE	FALSE

You're competitive.

TRUE	FALSE

What would surprise people to hear about you?

_____

_____

_____

_____

_____

_____

What's the worst lie you've ever told?

_____

_____

_____

_____

_____

_____

Who have you disappointed?

_____

_____

_____

_____

_____

_____

Are there conspiracy theories you think are true?

_____

_____

_____

_____

_____

_____

_____

Are you close to your family? Why or why not?

_____

_____

_____

_____

_____

_____

_____

If you could, which emotion would you bottle up and sell?

_____

_____

_____

_____

_____

_____

_____

What do you say when someone asks you to tell them about yourself?

_____

_____

_____

_____

_____

_____

_____

_____

_____

_____

Do you know the story of the day you were born?

_____

_____

_____

_____

_____

_____

_____

_____

_____

_____

_____

What do you like to do on your birthday?

_____

_____

_____

_____

_____

_____

_____

_____

_____

What's your idea of the perfect day?

_____

_____

_____

_____

_____

_____

_____

_____

_____

_____

_____

Do you like change?

_____

_____

_____

_____

_____

_____

_____

_____

_____

_____

What are you most grateful for today?

_____

_____

_____

_____

_____

_____

_____

_____

_____

_____

Has a song ever made you cry? Why?

_____

_____

_____

_____

_____

_____

_____

_____

_____

What do you have unwavering faith in?

_____

_____

_____

_____

_____

_____

_____

_____

_____

_____

_____

Comfort Items

What are your go-to comfort items when you've had a bad day?

Comfort Movie	
Comfort Book	
Comfort Food	
Comfort Drink	
Comfort Music	
Comfort Activity	

Happy Items

What are your go-to items when you're happy?

Happy Movie	
Happy Book	
Happy Food	
Happy Drink	
Happy Music	
Happy Activity	

How do you show people you care?

_____

_____

_____

_____

_____

_____

_____

_____

_____

_____

What's the one thing you would tell people to always do?

_____

_____

_____

_____

_____

_____

_____

_____

_____

_____

What's one thing you've always wanted to learn?

_____

_____

_____

_____

_____

_____

_____

_____

_____

Do you have any regrets?

_____

_____

_____

_____

_____

_____

_____

_____

_____

Who do you trust the most?

_____

_____

_____

_____

_____

_____

_____

_____

_____

Do you like your life at home?

_____

_____

_____

_____

_____

_____

_____

_____

_____

_____

When have you ever gone against the grain?

_____

_____

_____

_____

_____

_____

_____

_____

_____

Have you ever walked away from something or someone because it wasn't right for you?

_____

_____

_____

_____

_____

_____

_____

_____

_____

_____

Who I Am

On a scale of 1 to 10, how well do these personality traits describe you?
1 being not at all and 10 being very accurate.

Principled

1	2	3	4	5	6	7	8	9	10

Generous

1	2	3	4	5	6	7	8	9	10

Temperamental

1	2	3	4	5	6	7	8	9	10

Innovative

1	2	3	4	5	6	7	8	9	10

Suspicious

1	2	3	4	5	6	7	8	9	10

Spontaneous

1	2	3	4	5	6	7	8	9	10

Competitive

1	2	3	4	5	6	7	8	9	10

Decisive

1	2	3	4	5	6	7	8	9	10

Perceptive

1	2	3	4	5	6	7	8	9	10

Ambitious

1	2	3	4	5	6	7	8	9	10

Stubborn

1	2	3	4	5	6	7	8	9	10

Sensitive

1	2	3	4	5	6	7	8	9	10

Would You Rather?

Go on a perpetual road trip **OR** take four consecutive flights?

Live in space **OR** live in the ocean?

See ten minutes into the future **OR** time travel ten years into the past?

Watch only your favorite movie forever **OR** watch a movie you hate once a week?

Be able to control fire **OR** water?

Eat melted ice cream **OR** cold chili?

Wear the same color every day **OR** the same style of shirt every day?

Give up coffee **OR** give up soda?

Talk only in song **OR** only in whispers?

Ride a T-Rex **OR** fly on a Pterodactyl?

Get lost in Atlantis **OR** the Bermuda Triangle?

Be a Greek god **OR** a Roman god?

Bike everywhere **OR** only be able to take public transportation?

Be a world-famous magician but none of your magic is real **OR** a small-town magician, but all of your magic is real?

Go to the beach during a hurricane **OR** the mountains during a blizzard?

	OR	
Be in a 90s coming of age movie		an 80s horror movie?
Write books		make movies?
Be able to teleport		move things with your mind?
Never ever have to sleep again		always get a perfect eight hours?
Have perfect eyesight		perfect hearing?
Put cheese on everything		sugar on everything?
Be a ghost		werewolf?
Have unlimited sushi		unlimited pizza?
Have one free international trip every		fly domestically everywhere for free?
Lose all your hair		all your teeth?
Get up at 6am every day		stay up until 2am every night?
Only be able to write in red ink		never be able to use pens again?
Live in Victorian England		ancient Egypt?
Have no plumbing		no electricity?
Be a knight		a Viking?
Spend the day in Paris		in Rome?

What's your favorite way to travel? Car, train, or plane?

_____

_____

_____

_____

_____

_____

What kind of animal would you be?

_____

_____

_____

_____

_____

_____

What is one thing from your home you value most?

_____

_____

_____

_____

_____

_____

Do you prefer the heat or the cold?

_____

_____

_____

_____

_____

_____

_____

What's the best present you've ever received?

_____

_____

_____

_____

_____

_____

_____

If you could move anywhere, where would you move?

_____

_____

_____

_____

_____

_____

_____

What's one thing you cannot get enough of?

_____

_____

_____

_____

_____

_____

_____

_____

_____

What's the best feeling in the world?

_____

_____

_____

_____

_____

_____

_____

_____

_____

_____

What process do you enjoy most?

_____

_____

_____

_____

_____

_____

_____

_____

_____

Do you have a favorite city?

_____

_____

_____

_____

_____

_____

_____

_____

_____

_____

_____

What's the easiest thing you've done?

_____

_____

_____

_____

_____

_____

_____

_____

_____

When you stand in front of a mirror, what do you see?

_____

_____

_____

_____

_____

_____

_____

_____

_____

_____

Do you believe in luck?

_____

_____

_____

_____

_____

_____

_____

_____

_____

_____

How would you want to talk about the love of your life?

_____

_____

_____

_____

_____

_____

_____

_____

_____

_____

_____

A Little History

"Till this moment
I never knew myself."

—JANE AUSTEN

Confessions

Top five most embarrassing moments from your childhood/adolescence:

1. _____
   _____
   _____

2. _____
   _____
   _____

3. _____
   _____
   _____

4. _____
   _____
   _____

5. _____
   _____
   _____

Memories

Top five most memorable experiences from your childhood/adolescence:

1. _____
   _____
   _____

2. _____
   _____
   _____

3. _____
   _____
   _____

4. _____
   _____
   _____

5. _____
   _____
   _____

What was your favorite book as a child?

_____

_____

_____

_____

_____

_____

_____

_____

_____

_____

What's the most rebellious thing you did as a teenager?

_____

_____

_____

_____

_____

_____

_____

_____

_____

_____

Who was your first crush?

_____

_____

_____

_____

_____

_____

_____

_____

_____

What was your first heartbreak?

_____

_____

_____

_____

_____

_____

_____

_____

_____

_____

What's the one thing you've always wanted to say?

Did you ever learn something and then wished you never learned it?

Have you ever wasted someone's time?

_____

_____

_____

_____

_____

_____

_____

_____

_____

_____

When was the last time you were lonely?

_____

_____

_____

_____

_____

_____

_____

_____

_____

_____

_____

What's the deepest conversation you've ever had with a stranger?

_____

_____

_____

_____

_____

_____

_____

_____

_____

_____

If you could make something in your life automatic, what would it be?

_____

_____

_____

_____

_____

_____

_____

_____

_____

_____

What's one of the most beautiful things you've seen?

Who do you know that hasn't changed? Is that a good thing?

Teacher's Pet

We've all had at least one teacher that we'll never forget and made an impact in our life. Write about your favorite teachers.

Elementary School:

_____

_____

_____

_____

_____

Middle School:

_____

_____

_____

_____

_____

High School:

_____

_____

_____

_____

_____

BFFs

Write about the friends you had throughout your school years.

Elementary School:

_____

_____

_____

_____

_____

Middle School:

_____

_____

_____

_____

_____

High School:

_____

_____

_____

_____

_____

HISTORY

Have you ever helped someone in need?

_____

_____

_____

_____

_____

_____

_____

_____

_____

_____

Who did you used to know really well?

_____

_____

_____

_____

_____

_____

_____

_____

_____

_____

_____

Have you ever envied someone?

_____

_____

_____

_____

_____

_____

_____

_____

_____

What do most people want that you don't?

_____

_____

_____

_____

_____

_____

_____

_____

_____

_____

_____

Have you ever realized that someone from your past was right?

_____

_____

_____

_____

_____

_____

_____

_____

_____

What's been the most significant moment in your life?

_____

_____

_____

_____

_____

_____

_____

_____

_____

_____

What's the most fun party you've ever been to?

_____

_____

_____

_____

_____

_____

_____

_____

_____

If you could go back and start something again, what would it be?

_____

_____

_____

_____

_____

_____

_____

_____

_____

_____

HISTORY

Past Life

Check off everything you did as a child or teen.

☐ Played a sport

☐ Danced in a ballet recital

☐ Learned to play an instrument

☐ Failed a test

☐ Created a science experiment

☐ Stayed up all night working on a project

☐ Got stuck doing a group project by yourself

☐ Ran for student council

☐ Ditched school

☐ Wrote notes to someone during class

☐ Got detention

☐ Participated in a spelling bee

☐ Got your first pet

☐ Lost your homework

....

☐ Told someone you liked them

☐ Learned how to drive

☐ Lied to your parents

☐ Starred in a play

☐ Lost your first tooth at school

☐ Won a trophy or award

☐ Went to prom

☐ Went on your first date

☐ Wore a uniform

☐ Started your first job

☐ Joined the marching band

☐ Broke a bone

☐ Went to a sleepover

☐ Snuck out of your house

☐ Swapped lunches with a friend

HISTORY

What was elementary school like for you?

_____

_____

_____

_____

_____

_____

What was middle school like for you?

_____

_____

_____

_____

_____

_____

What was high school like for you?

_____

_____

_____

_____

_____

_____

What's something you liked to wear when you were younger?

_____

_____

_____

_____

_____

_____

What did you look forward to when you were a child?

_____

_____

_____

_____

_____

_____

What were your summer vacations like when you were younger?

_____

_____

_____

_____

_____

_____

_____

What should every child experience before they are ten years old?

What are some things you didn't understand as a child about being an adult but now you do?

_____

_____

_____

_____

_____

_____

_____

_____

_____

_____

_____

_____

_____

_____

_____

_____

_____

_____

_____

_____

_____

_____

_____

Three Words

Write down the first three words that come to mind when reading the words below. Don't think!

Parents

1.
2.
3.

School

1.
2.
3.

Friends

1.
2.
3.

Math

1.
2.
3.

Playground

1.
2.
3.

Recess

1.
2.
3.

Quick! Pick your childhood favorites of these duos. No thinking – go with your first impulse.

	OR	
Cookies		Cake
Birthday party		Birthday gifts
Juice		Chocolate milk
Chips		Crackers
Sweet		Sour
Mac and cheese		Chicken nuggets
Christmas		Summer
Pool		Beach
Video games		Board games
Skateboard		Roller skate
Amusement Park		Arcade
Vanilla		Chocolate
Ice cream		Milkshake
Pizza		Burger

Mix Tape

Make a playlist of your favorite teenage songs.

1.	
2.	
3.	
4.	
5.	
6.	
7.	
8.	
9.	
10.	
11.	
12.	
13.	
14.	
15.	

What is something you were afraid of before but aren't today?

_____

_____

_____

_____

_____

_____

_____

_____

_____

_____

_____

What's the biggest lie you've ever told?

_____

_____

_____

_____

_____

_____

_____

_____

_____

_____

_____

_____

Has anyone ever spread a rumor about you?

_____

_____

_____

_____

_____

_____

_____

_____

_____

_____

What's something you've done that's hurt someone's feelings?

_____

_____

_____

_____

_____

_____

_____

_____

_____

_____

Do you remember the first time you were on a plane? What was it like?

_____

_____

_____

_____

_____

_____

_____

_____

_____

What's a memory that makes you sad?

_____

_____

_____

_____

_____

_____

_____

_____

_____

_____

When's the last time you saw a sunset?

What was your favorite game while growing up?

Did you go to prom? What was it like?

_____

_____

_____

_____

_____

_____

_____

_____

_____

Can you describe your childhood bedroom?

_____

_____

_____

_____

_____

_____

_____

_____

_____

_____

What was your experience learning to ride a bike?

_____

_____

_____

_____

_____

_____

_____

_____

_____

What's the best holiday you've ever had?

_____

_____

_____

_____

_____

_____

_____

_____

_____

My First...

First concert:

_____

_____

_____

_____

_____

First party:

_____

_____

_____

_____

_____

First memory:

_____

_____

_____

_____

_____

First pet:

_____

_____

_____

_____

_____

First vacation:

_____

_____

_____

_____

_____

First school:

_____

_____

_____

_____

_____

HISTORY

What was your high school graduation like?

_____

_____

_____

_____

_____

_____

_____

What was your favorite subject in high school?

_____

_____

_____

_____

_____

_____

_____

What pets did you have?

_____

_____

_____

_____

_____

_____

_____

Were you a mischievous child?

_____

_____

_____

_____

_____

_____

_____

What's the one thing you never wanted to share as a child?

_____

_____

_____

_____

_____

_____

_____

Were you lonely as a child?

_____

_____

_____

_____

_____

_____

_____

What kind of adult did you think you would be?

_____

_____

_____

_____

_____

_____

_____

What dreams did you have about being an adult?

_____

_____

_____

_____

_____

_____

_____

In what ways are you still the same as when you were younger?

_____

_____

_____

_____

_____

_____

_____

In what ways are you different from when you were younger?

_____

_____

_____

_____

_____

_____

_____

What were your favorite outdoor activities?

_____

_____

_____

_____

_____

_____

What were your favorite indoor activities?

_____

_____

_____

_____

_____

_____

_____

Did you have a big imagination as a child?

_____

_____

_____

_____

_____

_____

_____

_____

_____

_____

What's the best feedback you've ever received?

_____

_____

_____

_____

_____

_____

_____

_____

_____

_____

What was your favorite candy growing up? Is there a memory attached to it?

_____

_____

_____

_____

_____

_____

_____

_____

_____

_____

When you were a child, who was your favorite relative?

_____

_____

_____

_____

_____

_____

_____

_____

_____

_____

_____

Time Machine

If you could go back in time and talk to yourself as a child, what would you say? What advice would you give?

If you could go back in time and talk to yourself as a teen, what would you say? What advice would you give?

_____

_____

_____

_____

_____

_____

_____

_____

_____

_____

_____

_____

_____

_____

_____

_____

_____

_____

_____

_____

_____

_____

What's the one thing you always did on Saturday mornings when you were a child?

_____

_____

_____

_____

_____

_____

_____

_____

_____

How do you feel when you see old videos of yourself?

_____

_____

_____

_____

_____

_____

_____

_____

_____

What's your favorite memory of playing outside as a child?

_____

_____

_____

_____

_____

_____

_____

_____

What's been the best year of your life so far?

_____

_____

_____

_____

_____

_____

_____

_____

What are the kinds of moments you tend to recall easily?

_____

_____

_____

_____

_____

_____

_____

_____

_____

_____

Has there been a time in your life when many things changed rapidly? How did that make you feel?

_____

_____

_____

_____

_____

_____

_____

_____

_____

_____

What do you miss the most about your childhood?

_____

_____

_____

_____

_____

_____

_____

_____

_____

_____

Who was a good influence in your life growing up?

_____

_____

_____

_____

_____

_____

_____

_____

_____

_____

_____

True or False

You've always had many friends.

TRUE	FALSE

You liked school.

TRUE	FALSE

You have a big family.

TRUE	FALSE

You were the class clown.

TRUE	FALSE

You were a theater kid.

TRUE	FALSE

You were homeschooled.

TRUE	FALSE

You're the middle child.

TRUE	FALSE

You were close to your grandparents.

TRUE	FALSE

You lived in many different places.

TRUE	FALSE

Your family is religious.

TRUE	FALSE

You went on many family vacations.

TRUE	FALSE

You like playing board games.

TRUE	FALSE

Did you ever want to be a foreign exchange student? Why?

_____

_____

_____

_____

_____

_____

_____

_____

_____

_____

What sports did you play?

_____

_____

_____

_____

_____

_____

_____

_____

_____

_____

_____

Who helped you when you were a high school student?
What do you remember about it?

_____

_____

_____

_____

_____

_____

_____

_____

_____

Did you participate in any clubs?

_____

_____

_____

_____

_____

_____

_____

_____

_____

What did you enjoy doing the most as a child?

What did you want to be when you grew up?

What's your most memorable birthday?

_____

_____

_____

_____

_____

_____

_____

_____

_____

_____

Who had the greatest impact on you as a child?

_____

_____

_____

_____

_____

_____

_____

_____

_____

_____

_____

Looking Forward to the Future

"Live! Live the wonderful life that is in you!
Let nothing be lost upon you.
Be always searching for new sensations.
Be afraid of nothing."

—OSCAR WILDE

What does your dream house look like?

_____

_____

_____

_____

_____

_____

_____

How would you want to change the world?

_____

_____

_____

_____

_____

_____

_____

Do you get overwhelmed planning the future?

_____

_____

_____

_____

_____

_____

_____

What are your future hopes and dreams?

_____

_____

_____

_____

_____

_____

_____

Where do you see yourself in ten years?

_____

_____

_____

_____

_____

_____

_____

What would you include in a time capsule?

_____

_____

_____

_____

_____

_____

_____

THE FUTURE

What inspires you to be daring?

_____

_____

_____

_____

_____

_____

_____

_____

_____

_____

Do you believe an older person is always wise?

_____

_____

_____

_____

_____

_____

_____

_____

_____

_____

_____

If you had to get a tattoo, what would it be?

What do you believe would change the course of a person's life?

What is something that you've put behind you? Why?

Do you think education can change the world?

What part of your life do you want to make a bigger effort in?

_____

_____

_____

_____

_____

_____

_____

_____

_____

What makes you feel motivated?

_____

_____

_____

_____

_____

_____

_____

_____

_____

_____

Confessions

Top five concerns about the future:

1.

2.

3.

4.

5.

Excitement

Top five things you're most excited about for the future:

1.

2.

3.

4.

5.

How do you feel about aging?

_____

_____

_____

_____

_____

_____

_____

_____

_____

_____

Would you dye your hair if it's too gray?

_____

_____

_____

_____

_____

_____

_____

_____

_____

_____

What is something you want to start collecting?

_____

_____

_____

_____

_____

_____

_____

_____

_____

_____

What types of friends do you want to have when you're older?

_____

_____

_____

_____

_____

_____

_____

_____

_____

_____

_____

_____

What defines your generation?

_____

_____

_____

_____

_____

_____

_____

_____

_____

_____

What's a goal everyone should have, even if they don't accomplish it?

_____

_____

_____

_____

_____

_____

_____

_____

_____

_____

_____

Describe the best version of yourself.

_____

_____

_____

_____

_____

_____

_____

_____

_____

_____

How would you want people to describe how your life progressed?

_____

_____

_____

_____

_____

_____

_____

_____

_____

_____

_____

_____

THE FUTURE

Future Me

Envision the life you want to be living in 20 years.

Describe where you live. What is the location like? What does your home look and feel like?

_____

_____

_____

_____

_____

_____

_____

_____

Describe the people in your life-family, friends, partner. What are your relationships like?

_____

_____

_____

_____

_____

_____

_____

_____

....

Describe your career. What kind of job do you have and how do you feel about it? How much money are you making? Or are you retired?

_____

_____

_____

_____

_____

_____

_____

_____

_____

Describe your hobbies and extracurriculars. How are you spending your time outside of work? Are you traveling a lot or learning something new? Are you pursuing the things that bring you joy?

_____

_____

_____

_____

_____

_____

_____

_____

THE FUTURE

What's something you would do if you won the lottery?

_____

_____

_____

_____

_____

_____

_____

_____

_____

_____

What's a story you're always going to tell once you're old?

_____

_____

_____

_____

_____

_____

_____

_____

_____

_____

If you could start your own business, what would it be?

How do your decisions now affect your future?

Do you believe that when people have what they want, they don't try anymore?

If you could make an investment, what would you invest in?

What would you build on a newly purchased piece of land? Why?

_____

_____

_____

_____

_____

_____

_____

_____

_____

What do you always leave for later?

_____

_____

_____

_____

_____

_____

_____

_____

_____

_____

_____

Three Words

Write down the first three words that come to mind when reading these below.

Future

1.
2.
3.

Career

1.
2.
3.

Retirement

1.
2.
3.

Dreams

1.	
2.	
3.	

Death

1.	
2.	
3.	

World

1.	
2.	
3.	

True or False

You want to be wealthy in the future.

TRUE	FALSE

You want to travel more.

TRUE	FALSE

You would like to be a grandparent.

TRUE	FALSE

You want to change careers.

TRUE	FALSE

You're confident you will achieve your goals.

TRUE	FALSE

You want to write a book.

TRUE	FALSE

You want to live in a different country.

TRUE	FALSE

You want to go back to school.

TRUE	FALSE

You need to make a huge life-altering decision.

TRUE	FALSE

You want to learn something new.

TRUE	FALSE

You want to pick up an old hobby again.

TRUE	FALSE

You want to become more active.

TRUE	FALSE

THE FUTURE

If you could invent anything, what would it be?

_____

_____

_____

_____

_____

_____

_____

Is there something you don't want to be afraid of anymore?

_____

_____

_____

_____

_____

_____

_____

Where do you see yourself tomorrow?

_____

_____

_____

_____

_____

_____

_____

What's the one thing you couldn't conceive ever happening?

_____

_____

_____

_____

_____

_____

_____

What do you think science will do in your lifetime?

_____

_____

_____

_____

_____

_____

_____

How do you measure your days?

_____

_____

_____

_____

_____

_____

_____

If you could take a drive anywhere, where would it be?

What's a mystery you wish you could solve?

Do you equate growth with maturity?

What's a celebration you want to attend in the future?

Time Machine

If you could travel to the future and talk to your future self, what do you think they would say to you? What advice or instructions would they give you?

What do you think your future self would warn you about?

My Eras

Describe all the eras of your life thus far.

Describe all of your future eras.

If you could have multiple professions, what would they be?

If you could learn to cook a specialty dish, who would be the best teacher?

What habits do you want to cultivate as you get older?

_____

_____

_____

_____

_____

_____

_____

_____

_____

_____

Do you feel like your life is moving forward or backward?

_____

_____

_____

_____

_____

_____

_____

_____

_____

_____

_____

What's something you still want to learn?

_____

_____

_____

_____

_____

_____

_____

_____

_____

What's a machine that should exist?

_____

_____

_____

_____

_____

_____

_____

_____

_____

What are your future priorities?

_____

_____

_____

_____

_____

_____

_____

_____

_____

_____

After you retire, what do you want people to say about you at work?

_____

_____

_____

_____

_____

_____

_____

_____

_____

_____

_____

Do you believe there's a specific age one can do things?

_____

_____

_____

_____

_____

_____

_____

_____

_____

What's one action you could take today to make you happy?

_____

_____

_____

_____

_____

_____

_____

_____

_____

_____

What amount of money would make you quit your job?

_____

_____

_____

_____

_____

_____

_____

_____

What is the last thing you almost did? What stopped you?

_____

_____

_____

_____

_____

_____

_____

_____

_____

_____

Bucket List

Check off what you've already done from this bucket list and keep it handy to check off items in the future!

- [ ] Go scuba diving

- [ ] Go bungee jumping

- [ ] Visit a new country

- [ ] Hike in a national park

- [ ] See the Northern Lights in person

- [ ] Learn a new language

- [ ] Ride in a hot air balloon

- [ ] Meet someone famous

- [ ] Take an art class

- [ ] Win a contest

- [ ] Learn to play an instrument

....

Now create your own bucket list.

☐ _____

☐ _____

☐ _____

☐ _____

☐ _____

☐ _____

☐ _____

☐ _____

☐ _____

☐ _____

☐ _____

THE FUTURE

Is there a goal you've put off in accomplishing?

_____

_____

_____

_____

_____

_____

_____

_____

_____

_____

If you were to devote yourself to something, what would it be?

_____

_____

_____

_____

_____

_____

_____

_____

_____

_____

What's one thing you've always wanted?

_____

_____

_____

_____

_____

_____

_____

_____

Are there any grudges you want to let go?

_____

_____

_____

_____

_____

_____

_____

_____

_____

_____

If you could build a house anywhere would you do it on a tropical island or in the middle of a forest?

_____

_____

_____

_____

_____

_____

_____

_____

_____

_____

What's a challenge you've always wanted to overcome?

_____

_____

_____

_____

_____

_____

_____

_____

_____

_____

If you had to choose between living in a city or a rural area forever, what would you choose? Why?

_____

_____

_____

_____

_____

_____

_____

_____

_____

_____

Who would you put in charge of the world if it had to be one person?

_____

_____

_____

_____

_____

_____

_____

_____

_____

_____

_____

THE FUTURE

What is the one bad thing you would eliminate from the world?

If you could be known for turning a bill into a law, what would it be?

What should everyone consider when they make a decision?

_____

_____

_____

_____

_____

_____

_____

_____

_____

What advice would you give someone in the darkest time of their life?

_____

_____

_____

_____

_____

_____

_____

_____

_____

_____

_____

Rapid Fire

Quick! Pick your favorites of these duos. No thinking – go with your first impulse.

Flying cars		Self-driving cars
Hot drinks		Cold drinks
Planes		Trains
E-books		Audiobooks
Soda		Sparkling water
Breakfast		Dinner
Minimalism	OR	Maximalism
Desert		Forest
Shower		Bath
Take out		Dine out
Pancake		Waffle
Cupcakes		Donuts

Phone call	Text
Pasta	Ramen
Pop music	Rock music
Rain	Snow
Sunrise	Sunset
Football	Baseball
Neutral	Colorful
Fries	Onion Rings
Bagels	Muffins
Cards	Crossword Puzzles
Ski	Snowboard
Movie	Book

OR

Do you like change?

_____

_____

_____

_____

_____

_____

_____

_____

_____

_____

If you were given the choice to live forever, would you do it?

_____

_____

_____

_____

_____

_____

_____

_____

_____

_____

_____

What keeps you up at night?

_____

_____

_____

_____

_____

_____

_____

_____

_____

_____

Do you think your definition of love will change?

_____

_____

_____

_____

_____

_____

_____

_____

_____

_____

_____

Do you believe people are born with a set destiny or do we have the power to change it?

How do you want to evolve professionally?

If you could be an expert on something, what would it be?

_____

_____

_____

_____

_____

_____

_____

_____

_____

If you had the money, what would you fund indefinitely?

_____

_____

_____

_____

_____

_____

_____

_____

_____

_____

_____

If you could go on any adventure, what would you choose?

_____

_____

_____

_____

_____

_____

_____

_____

_____

If there was a list called "New Me" what would you add to it?

_____

_____

_____

_____

_____

_____

_____

_____

_____

_____

What's the one thing that you could accomplish that would make you feel like you don't need to accomplish anything else?

_____

_____

_____

_____

_____

_____

_____

_____

_____

What's the one thing you could add to your life today to make it better?

_____

_____

_____

_____

_____

_____

_____

_____

My Legacy

What do you want your legacy to be? How do you want to be remembered?

What's a challenge you want to overcome?

_____

_____

_____

_____

_____

_____

_____

_____

_____

What's the next risk you want to take?

_____

_____

_____

_____

_____

_____

_____

_____

_____

_____

How can you become a better communicator?

_____

_____

_____

_____

_____

_____

_____

_____

_____

If you could redesign something, what would it be?

_____

_____

_____

_____

_____

_____

_____

_____

_____

_____

_____

THE FUTURE

What makes you feel motivated?

_____

_____

_____

_____

_____

_____

_____

_____

_____

What is a full life?

_____

_____

_____

_____

_____

_____

_____

_____

_____

_____

What's something you're looking forward to?

_____

_____

_____

_____

_____

_____

_____

_____

_____

What's high on your list of things to consider when you move somewhere?

_____

_____

_____

_____

_____

_____

_____

_____

_____

_____

_____

THE FUTURE

What do you believe is the best thing about being human?

_____

_____

_____

_____

_____

_____

_____

_____

_____

_____

If you could leave a message to a future generation, what would it be?

_____

_____

_____

_____

_____

_____

_____

_____

_____

_____

_____

_____

What do you consider to be a good opportunity?

_____

_____

_____

_____

_____

_____

_____

_____

_____

How can you be a better participant in your community?

_____

_____

_____

_____

_____

_____

_____

_____

_____

_____

_____

THE FUTURE

Future Predictions

Look ahead and write down what you see for your future.